THIS JOURNAL BELONGS TO:

Yay All Day

Printed in China

SPRUCE BOOKS with colophon is a registered
trademark of Penguin Random House LLC

25 24 23 22 21   9 8 7 6 5 4 3 2 1

Text: Asha Myers
Illustrations: Courtney Cook
Editor: Jill Saginario
Production editor: Bridget Sweet
Designer: Alicia Terry

ISBN: 978-1-63217-385-0

Sasquatch Books
1904 Third Avenue, Suite 710
Seattle, WA 98101

SasquatchBooks.com

Yay All Day

Good News Journal

Asha Myers

Illustrated by **Courtney Cook**

SPRUCE BOOKS
A Sasquatch Books Imprint

INTRODUCTION

Yay All Day is a fizzy and sugary anthem of delight for those who believe humans are more creative, more kind, and more powerful than all the problems they face. It's a belief in the power of positivity, and—let's be real—positivity takes guts.

Guts is looking a scary problem in the eye and seeing possibility. Guts is watching the world crumble and calling it progress.

It isn't delusional to smile at thunderclouds; there really is a rainbow hiding in there! Just like it isn't silly to choose optimism in the face of hardship; there really is opportunity hiding in there. Current research tells us that optimists are the most resilient people, meaning that the tough times don't bury them—they bounce back and actually feel more good feelings than those who can't find meaning in the obstacle. In fact, just reading about positive things energizes us and makes us happier!

For any positivity-parched soul, this book is a thirst quencher.

When you need an infusion of hope, turn to these refreshing stories, which highlight how people use their brilliance and flair, their brains and their gumption, to spark light and hope in the lives of others. The stories celebrate simple ways to overcome adversity with silliness, sweetness, and sass. And take heart from the power of stories that prove we all have something to give.

Use the journal pages to explore all your emotions. Write about the good, the bad, the ugly, and the awesome. Transform anything you don't like into something you do. Take what excites you and see if there's a way to have more of it in your life. Let the good news stories inspire you to leave your own special fingerprint on someone else's life. Someone else could be a person, an animal, a honeybee, or a rain forest. That's for you to decide.

6

Just like this thousand-year-old cherry tree, you too can bloom through disasters of all kinds. She has survived wars, earthquakes, a nuclear disaster, and pandemics, yet year after year she shares the most gorgeous and fragrant blossoms with all the travelers who come to visit her. The tree's caretaker says the tree reminds us that we too, just like she, "will see more bad things, but she'll also see good—life is layers, layers of bad and good."

The world needs bold people willing to keep blooming— to keep sharing their unique sparkle and flavor with the world. You are a bold person. And if you don't believe it yet, maybe by the end of this journal you will.

Will you be audacious in your imagination? Will you be unflappably optimistic? Will you be relentless in your search for the good at the heart of all things? Of course you will, because you've got guts, and the world needs the lifesaving positivity only you can bring.

My superpower is to make you smile.

Two teens dressed in spandex superhero outfits do random acts of kindness to prove it doesn't take super strength or super speed to change someone's life for the better.

We all possess the power to do good.

They say manta rays only come in black or white. But, surprise! The world's one and only known hot-pink manta ray proves there is no one right way to survive and thrive in this world. Diversity is the spice of life. Go ahead—live life in your own personal neon shimmer.

13

Burkina Faso teenager Mariama Mamane fights for the future by finding the opportunity within the problem. She takes water hyacinth, an invasive species, and turns it into "energy for all" as organic fertilizer and electricity from biogas.

Say pasta la vista to plastic straws!
Italy is solving the plastic waste
crisis with biodegradable, flavorless,
edible, and *strong* pasta straws.
Now that's *amore*!

21

Smile!

29

COVID-19 doesn't stand a chance against a dog's schnoz! In Alfort, France, researchers found that trained dogs are 95 percent successful at detecting the virus, even in people with no symptoms. They just, uh, need to sniff our armpits. But hey! It's good news for airport security and other busy places to help slow the spread.

You've got to be kitten me! Cut that out right meow—
like how one art vigilante in England protests that
rubbish by slapping cat stickers over it.

The Rainbow Railroad creates paths to safety for persecuted LGBTQI+ people from around the world!

Since 2006, they have helped over eight hundred individuals escape hostile environments and find new homes in countries that celebrate diversity and love in all its forms.

41

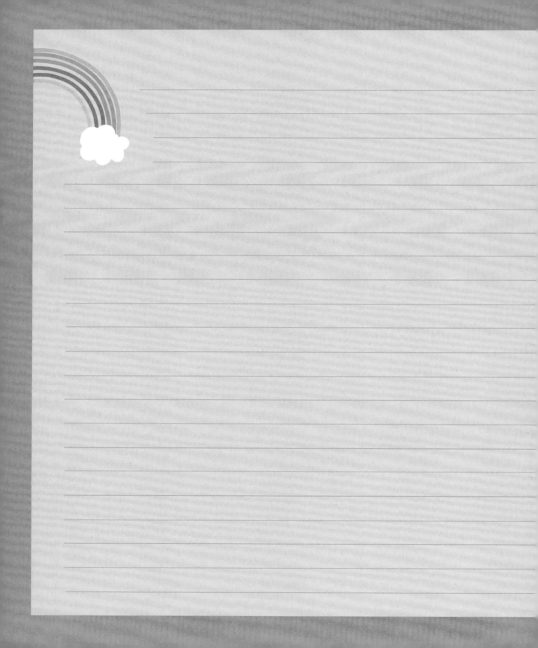

A student stitched up very fetching bow ties for his pet-obsessed teachers who were having a "ruff" time during the 2020 school shutdowns, giving them at least one reason to laugh each day.

Protests work, and reform is possible!
Colorado becomes the first state to
pass a sweeping police reform bill that
bans choke holds, prohibits shooting
at fleeing suspects, and holds police
officers financially liable for violating
a person's civil rights.

Costa Rica reversed their deforestation, and 99.5 percent of their energy now comes from clean and renewable sources! "You could say that Costa Rica is so small, no matter what they do, it won't have an impact on global emissions. But what is done in Costa Rica proves that it is possible."

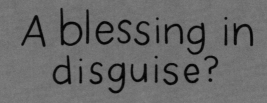

A blessing in disguise?

Priest becomes a "masked avenger"
on Easter during the COVID-19
pandemic and squirts holy water
at parishioners while they
drive by in cars.

Humpback whales band together to save animals from killer-whale attacks, sometimes even cuddling seals and rolling them out of the water to make a rescue. This humpback saved a diver by shielding her from a tiger shark and nudging her toward her boat. Hurray for the bold action that brought these heroes of the sea back from the brink of extinction!

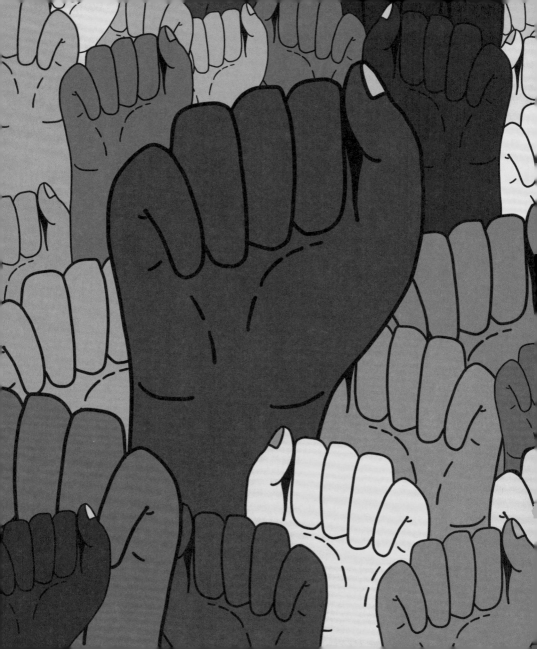

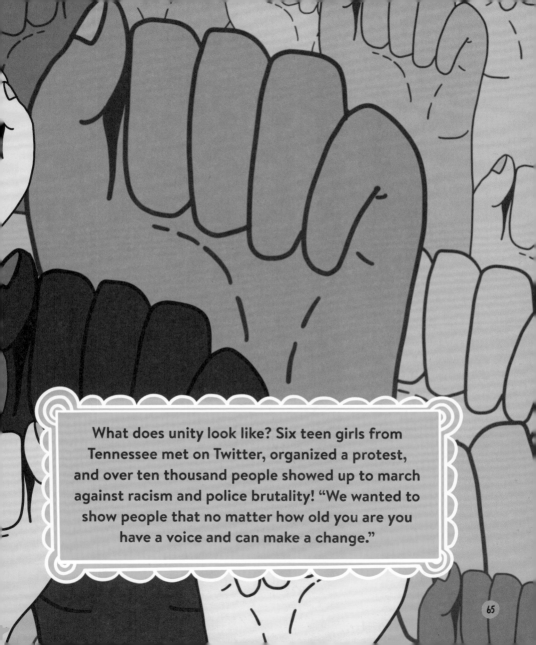

What does unity look like? Six teen girls from Tennessee met on Twitter, organized a protest, and over ten thousand people showed up to march against racism and police brutality! "We wanted to show people that no matter how old you are you have a voice and can make a change."

Fighting COVID-19 and prejudice,

one gay couple handed out rainbow face masks in Poland (where homosexuality is considered a plague), "proving that an infectious disease like discrimination stands no chance in the face of a guerrilla kindness campaign."

Transgender navy officer wins exception to the trans military ban, allowing her to serve in her true gender. This victory paves the way for other transgender patriots to serve openly and authentically.

You've got the beat! Israeli scientists prove that when people drum together,

their hearts beat in sync.

Turns out, when our hearts beat in sync with others, we feel a deep sense of belonging and connection, and those are the exact feelings we need to work together to change the world for the better!

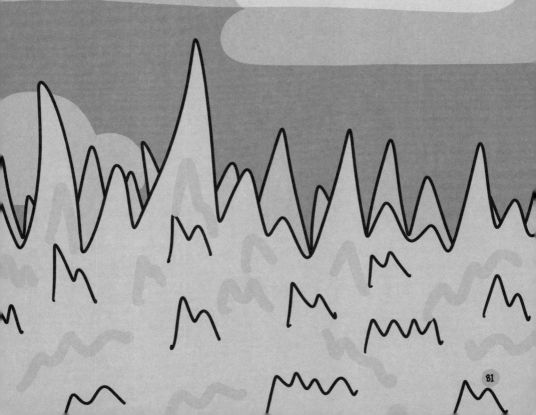

Philadelphia teen Dejour Williams wants teens to know we each have the power to help others help themselves. Dejour used the money he earned from his lawn-mowing business to buy a new mower for a homeless man, giving the man an opportunity to start his own business and break the cycle of poverty.

On February 14, 2020, a teenage boy brought 170 flowers to school so every girl would have a valentine. His reason? He didn't "want anyone to feel less important than anyone else."

Los Angeles builds a giant bridge across a ten-lane highway to save endangered mountain lions.

They (and other wildlife!) will use this "bridge of love" to safely cross into new mountain territory and find their special someone to mate with.

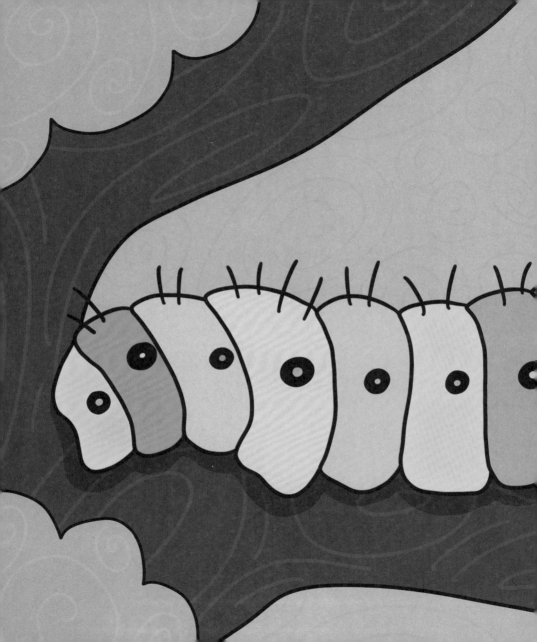

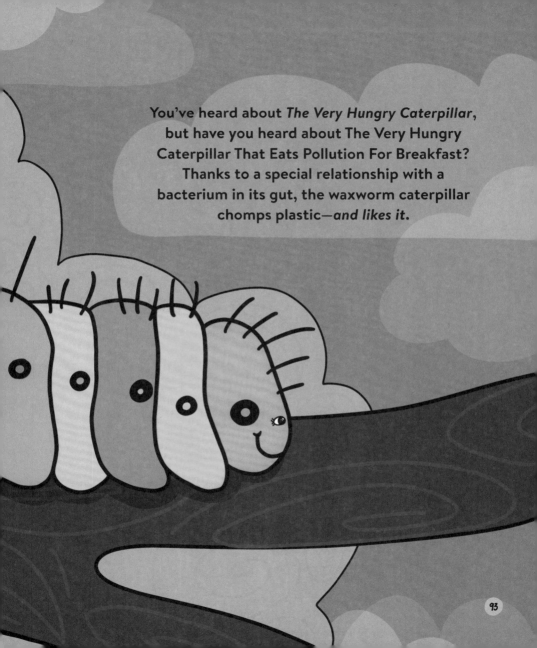

You've heard about *The Very Hungry Caterpillar*, but have you heard about The Very Hungry Caterpillar That Eats Pollution For Breakfast? Thanks to a special relationship with a bacterium in its gut, the waxworm caterpillar chomps plastic—*and likes it.*

The Black Mambas, an all-woman anti-poaching team, have reduced illegal rhino poaching by 86 percent in the area they patrol. "They say it's a man's job, but we are doing it." They are so well trained that they not only reduce crime and survive in the wilderness—alongside lions, elephants, rhinos, and leopards—but they also do it *without carrying weapons*. True badassery.

There's always a clever solution! Teen designs
3D-printed weighted belts for injured sea turtles with
"bubble butt" syndrome, giving them back their ability
to dive for food and return to the wild.

Taking steps to honor the diversity of people who helped push the frontiers of space exploration, NASA renames its Washington, DC, headquarters after Mary W. Jackson, the first African American female engineer at NASA and one of three Black women who were essential to the success of early spaceflight.

Espresso yourself!

Sunglasses made from coffee are a stylish solution to petroleum plastic shades. (And bonus: bury them in your garden for a natural, planet-friendly fertilizer when you're ready for new ones!)

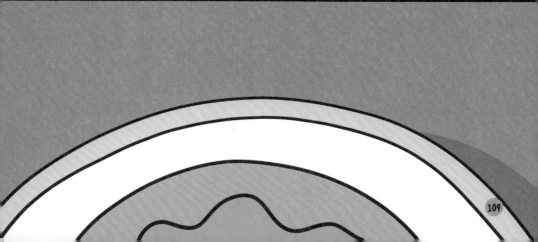

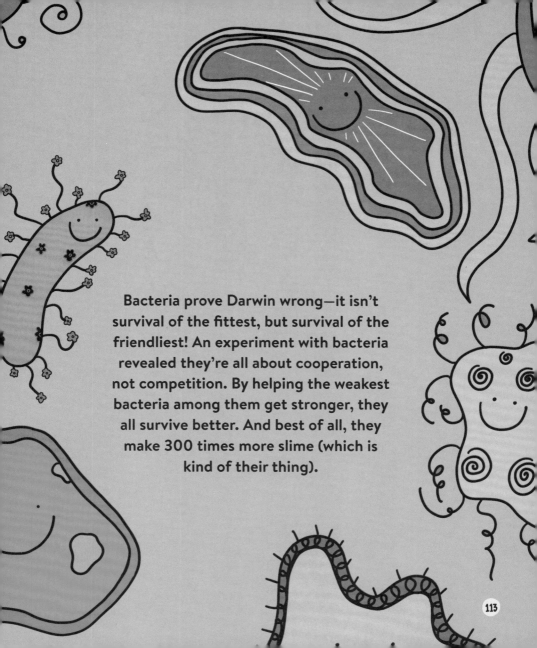

Bacteria prove Darwin wrong—it isn't survival of the fittest, but survival of the friendliest! An experiment with bacteria revealed they're all about cooperation, not competition. By helping the weakest bacteria among them get stronger, they all survive better. And best of all, they make 300 times more slime (which is kind of their thing).

A photographer captured two widowed penguins hugging and comforting each other while they watched the twinkle of city lights in the distance, and the whole social media world erupted in pen-grins at the incredible sweetness of it.

BIBLIOGRAPHY

PAGE 4: Smith, Emily Esfahani. "The Benefits of Optimism Are Real." *Atlantic*, March 2013. TheAtlantic.com.

PAGE 7: Corbley, McKinley. "This 1,000-Year-Old Cherry Tree in Japan Is a Role Model for Resilience During Trying Times." Good News Network, April 2020. GoodNewsNetwork.org.

PAGE 9: Hiddenreaction. "How to Be a Superhero." YouTube, December 2013. YouTube.com.

PAGE 12: Augliere, Bethany. "How Did This Rare Pink Manta Get Its Color?" *National Geographic*, February 2020. NationalGeographic.com.

PAGE 17: Fussstetter, Florian, producer. "Plant to Power in Burkina Faso." UN Environment Programme, July 2019. UNEP.org.

PAGE 21: Reddit post by GranFabio. "Here in Italy bars are starting to use pasta as straws to reduce plastic use. Our technology amazes the world another time." Reddit, September 2019. Reddit.com.

Stroodles Pasta Straws. "About Us." Stroodles.co.uk.

PAGE 24: Zaslow, Alexandra. "Siblings Give Up Birthday Presents to Make 900 Sandwiches to Feed the Homeless." *Today Show Online*, October 2015. Today.com.

PAGE 28: Richie, Hannah, and Max Roser. "Clean Water." *Our World in Data*, September 2019. OurWorldInData.org/Water-Access.

"Why Water?" Water.org, July 2020. Water.org.

PAGE 32: Brulliard, Karin. "Dogs Are Being Trained to Sniff Out Coronavirus Cases." *Washington Post*, April 2020. WashingtonPost.com.

Corbley, Andy. "Dogs Trained to Sniff Out COVID-19 Score Near-Perfect in Diagnosis of Human Sweat Samples." Good News Network, June 2020. GoodNewsNetwork.org.

PAGE 37: Aleksandrova, Dayana. "Manchester Art Vigilante Is Covering Racist Graffiti with Cat Stickers." Matador Network, May 2020. MatadorNetwork.com.

PAGE 40: Rainbow Railroad. "Who We Help." RainbowRailroad.org.

PAGE 45: @onlyrational. "My-bows. Once upon a time, we were in quarantine for COVID19. We had a sewing machine and fabric and time and a 12-year-old trying to figure out what to do with himself." Instagram, June 2020. Instagram.com.

PAGE 48: Cohen, Li. "Colorado Passes Sweeping Police Reform Bill." CBS News, June 2020. CBSNews.com.

Miller, Blair. "'We heard your cry': Colorado Governor Signs Sweeping Police Reform Bill Invigorated by Protests." The Denver Channel, June 2020. TheDenverChannel.com.

PAGE 53: UN Environment Programme, producer. "Champion of the Earth 2019: Costa Rica." YouTube, September 2019. YouTube.com.

PAGE 57: Diskin, Eben. "A Priest Is Using a Water Gun to Squirt Churchgoers with Holy Water from a Distance." Matador Network, May 2020. MatadorNetwork.com.

PAGE 60: Material provided by University of Washington. "Humpback Whale Population on the Rise after Near Miss with Extinction." Science Daily, October 2019. ScienceDaily.com.

Spektor, Brandon. "This Whale Saved a Woman's Life, but Probably Not on Purpose." LiveScience, January 2018. LiveScience.com.

PAGE 65: Wanshel, Elyse. "Teen Girls Organized a 10,000-Person Black Lives Matter Protest in Nashville." *HuffPost*, June 2020. HuffPost.com.

Alund, Natalie Neysa, Brinley Hineman, and Adam Tamburin. "Teenagers Join Pantheon of Nashville Youth Who Harnessed Peaceful Protests to Urge Change." *Tennessean*, June 2020. Tennessean.com.

Teens4Equality (@teens.4.equality). "Local Nashville students making a difference nationally." Instagram.com.

PAGE 69: Garry, John. "10 Good News Stories from the LGBTQ Community This April That Will Make You Smile." Matador Network, April 2020. MatadorNetwork.com.

PAGE 73: Ring, Trudy. "Transgender Navy Officer Wins Waiver to Serve Openly." *Advocate*, May 2020. Advocate.com.

PAGE 76: Materials provided by Bar-Ilan University. "Hearts That Drum Together Beat Together." ScienceDaily, May 2020. ScienceDaily.com.

PAGE 81: Reyes, Jeannette. "Philadelphia Teen's Good Deed Gives Homeless Man a Second Chance." ABC7 News, June 2018. ABC7news.com.

PAGE 85: Weaver, Anna. "Teen Bought 170 Flowers So He Could Give Every Girl at School a Valentine." Simplemost, February 2020. Simplemost.com.

PAGE 88: Douglas, Lucy. "Plan to Save LA's Mountain Lions—with a Big Bridge." *Positive News*, September 2019. Positive.news.

PAGE 93: Rosane, Olivia. "How a Plastic-Eating Caterpillar Could Help Solve the World's Waste Crisis." EcoWatch, March 2020. EcoWatch.com.

PAGE 97: Goyanes, Cristina. "These Badass Women Are Taking on Poachers—and Winning." *National Geographic*, November 2017. NationalGeographic.com.

PAGE 101: Brookshire, Bethany. "Teen Designs Belt to Hold Down a Sea Turtle's Bubble Butt." *Science News for Students,* May 2019. ScienceNewsforStudents.org.

PAGE 104: National Aeronautics and Space Administration. "NASA Names Headquarters After 'Hidden Figure' Mary W. Jackson." Press release no. 20-068, June 2020. NASA.gov.

PAGE 109: Todd, Craig J. "Smelling Good—the World's First Sunglasses Made from Coffee." *Eco Tech Daily,* September 2018. EcoTechDaily.net.

PAGE 113: Material provided by University of Copenhagen. "Bacteria Contradict Darwin: Survival of the Friendliest." Phys.org, October 2019. Phys.org.

PAGE 117: S, Sethuraman. "Photographer Captures Two Widowed Penguins Comforting Each Other in Touching Photos." Shared, April 2020. Life.Shared.com.

Matt (@dogfather). "couldn't stop thinking about these penguins enjoying the Melbourne skyline together so i found the original photographer and apparently they're BOTH WIDOWED i can't handle it." twitter.com/dogfather/status/1251772190825033729. Photo by Tobias Baumgaertner of TobiasVisuals.com.

Get Involved

GLOBAL GOALS: GlobalGoals.org

Learn about the seventeen Global Goals world leaders agreed upon to create a better world by 2030 and how you can get involved in the effort to end poverty, fight inequality, and address the urgency of climate change.

LITTLE BY LITTLE: YouTube.com/c/LittlebyLittle

"Little x Little (LxL) is a global campaign to support the United Nations Sustainable Development Goals. It started with a simple fact: right now, there are 2 billion fifteen- to twenty-four-year-olds on the planet. That is the largest generation in human history. Which means if they all did one thing, it would be the largest collection of positive acts ever assembled. All you have to do is record a single action, tag it #LittlexLittle, and watch it join 2 billion just like it."

NATIONAL WILDLIFE REFUGE SYSTEM: fws.gov/refuges

Help endangered species by volunteering your time at a local nature preserve or wildlife refuge. Use the website above to find the ones near you.

CONSERVATION NATION: ConservationNation.org

Learn how to host a fundraiser for endangered species! "Conservation Nation makes it easy for anyone to save endangered animals. We work directly with Smithsonian scientists and wildlife experts, funding the equipment and resources they need to make a difference for species around the world. By empowering everyone to directly impact the most critical conservation projects, we are creating a better future for ourselves, for wildlife, and for our planet."

ORGANIZE A PROTEST

Peaceful protests play a huge role in human rights movements around the world. Want to organize your own?

• Read this online article by the ACLU and familiarize yourself with your rights: "Know Your Rights: Protesters' Rights."

• And read this PDF by Amnesty International for how to stay safe: www.amnestyusa.org/pdfs/SafeyDuringProtest_F.pdf

• Finally, read the article by KaeLyn on Autostraddle.com that covers nine important things to know as you organize your protest: "Want to Organize a Protest? Here Are 9 Things You Need to Know."

have a great day!

ABOUT THE AUTHOR AND ILLUSTRATOR

ASHA MYERS lives in the beautiful Driftless region of Wisconsin where she writes books for children and teens. She likes walking, laughing, and finding hope in the most unlikely of places. Her favorite humans are her husband, Dave, and their sweet baby, June.

COURTNEY COOK is a writer, illustrator, teacher, and lover of naps. She received an MFA in creative nonfiction from the University of California, Riverside. She grew up in Winnetka, Illinois, and now resides in Chicago with her cat, Bertie.